GALE
CENGAGE Learning

Short Stories for Students, Volume 5

Staff

Editorial: Tim Akers, Jerry Moore, *Editors*. Tim Akers, Joseph Alvarez, James Aren, Christine G. Berg, Thomas Bertonneau, Cynthia Bily, Yoonmee Chang, Carol Dell' Amico, Catherine Dominic, Catherine V. Donaldson, Tom Faulkner, Angela Frattarola, Tanya Gardiner-Scott, Terry Girard, Diane Andrews Henningfeld, Richard Henry, Erik Huber, Kendall Johnson, Dustie Kellet, David Kippen, Rena Korb, Ondine Le Blanc, Jean Leverich, Sarah Madsen Hardy, Thomas March, Jerry Moore, Carl Mowery, Robert Peltier, Jane Phillips, Elisabeth Piedmont-Marton, Shaun Strohmer, *Sketchwriters*. Jeffrey W. Hunter, Daniel Jones, John D. Jorgenson, Deborah A. Schmitt, Polly Vedder, Timothy J. White, Kathleen Wilson, *Contributing Editors*. James P. Draper, *Managing Editor*.

Research: Victoria B. Cariappa, *Research Team*

Manager. Andrew Malonis, *Research Specialist.*

Permissions: Susan M. Trosky, *Permissions Manager.* Kimberly Smilay, *Permissions Specialist.* Kelly Quin, *Permissions Associate.*

Production: Mary Beth Trimper, *Production Director.* Evi Seoud, *Assistant Production Manager.* Shanna Heilveil, *Production Assistant.*

Graphic Services: Randy Bassett, *Image Database Supervisor.* Mikal Ansari, Robert Duncan, *Imaging Specialists.* Pamela A. Reed, *Photography Coordinator.*

Copyright Notice

Copyright 1999
The Gale Group
27500 Drake Road
Farmington Hills, MI 48331-3535

This book is printed on acid-free paper that meets the minimum requirements of American National Standard for Information Sciences—Permanence Paper for Printed Library Materials, ANSI Z39.48-1984.

ISBN 0-7876-2220-6
ISSN 1092-7735

Printed in the United States of America
10 9 8 7 6 5 4 3 2

Harrison Bergeron

Kurt Vonnegut 1961

Introduction

"Harrison Bergeron" was first published in the October, 1961, issue of the *Magazine of Fantasy and Science Fiction*. It was Vonnegut's third publication in a science fiction magazine following the drying up of the once-lucrative weekly family magazine market where he had published more than twenty stories between 1950 and 1961. The story did not receive any critical attention, however, until 1968 when it appeared in Vonnegut's collection *Welcome to the Monkey House*. Initial reviews of the collection generally were less than favorable, with even more positive reviewers, such as Mitchel Levitas in the *New York Times* and Charles Nicol in the *Atlantic Monthly,* commenting negatively on the commercial quality of many of the stories. By the late 1980s, however, "Harrison Bergeron" was being reprinted in high school and college literature anthologies. Popular aspects of the story include Vonnegut's satire of both enforced equality and the power of the Handicapper General, and the enervating effect television can have on viewers. "Harrison Bergeron" likely draws upon a controversial 1961 speech by then Federal Communications Commission chairman Newton Minow titled "The Vast Wasteland," a reference to a supposed dearth of quality in television programming. Coincidentally, "Harrison Bergeron" also alludes to the George Burns and Gracie Allen television show, a weekly situation comedy and variety show popular in the late 1950s and early 1960s. Vonnegut has said that he learned most of what he believes about social and political idealism from junior civics class, as well as from the democratic institution of the public school itself. A futuristic story dealing with universal themes of equality, freedom, power and its abuses, and media influence, "Harrison Bergeron" continues to evoke thoughtful responses about equality and individual freedom in the United States.

Author Biography

Kurt Vonnegut, Jr., was born in 1922, the youngest of three children of Edith and Kurt Vonnegut, in Indianapolis, Indiana. His siblings had attended private schools, but financial difficulties during the Great Depression meant that Vonnegut had to attend public schools. He has said that he gleaned the basis of his political and social beliefs from his junior civics class.

After graduation, Vonnegut attended Cornell University. In 1943, during World War II, he enlisted in the U. S. Army. In 1944, he was captured by German soldiers and sent to Dresden, Germany, where he survived the bombing raids of February, 1945. After the war, Vonnegut married Jane Cox and moved to Chicago where he worked as a newspaper reporter and attended the University of Chicago. However, he left Chicago for a public relations job with General Electric in Schenectady, New York, before completing his master's degree in anthropology.

While working for General Electric, Vonnegut sold his first story, "Report on the Barnhouse Effect," to *Collier's* magazine; it was published in 1950. With the money from the sale of that story and three others, he quit his job in 1951, moved to Cape Cod, and embarked on a career as a writer. To supplement his income, he wrote public relations copy, taught school, and sold automobiles. His first novel, *Player Piano,* appeared in 1952, followed by *The Sirens of Titan* in 1959; *Canary in a Cat House* (short story collection), 1961; *Mother Night,* 1962; *Cat's Cradle,* 1963; and *God Bless You, Mr. Rosewater,* 1964. *Welcome to the Monkey House,* which includes "Harrison Bergeron," was Vonnegut's second collection of stories and was published in 1968. In the mid-1960s, Vonnegut began to attract some critical attention, but he did not become a well-known author until the publication of *Slaughterhouse-Five* in 1969. His first marriage ended early in the 1970s, and he later married photographer Jill Krementz. The 1970s and 1980s saw the publication of six more of Vonnegut's novels, including *Breakfast of Champions* (1973), *Jailbird* (1979), and *Galapagos* (1985). He has also published a book of "opinions": *Wampeters, Foma, and Granfalloons* (1974); and two autobiographical books: *Palm Sunday* (1981), and *Fates Worse Than Death* (1991).

The acclaim which met the publication of *Slaughterhouse-Five* led to much public recognition for Vonnegut. He has become an outspoken defender of free speech and an eloquent attacker of censorship. His critical reputation has been uneven, however. While several books devoted to Vonnegut's work were published in the 1970s, Vonnegut's later works have not been as well received by scholars as his earlier novels. Early critical attention tried to determine whether Vonnegut was a satirist, a black humorist, or a science fiction writer; this debate continues. His works are noted for their frank and insightful social criticism, and for their innovative style; they present readers with an idiosyncratic yet compelling vision of modern life.

Plot Summary

"Harrison Bergeron" is set in the future, when Constitutional Amendments have made everyone equal. The agents of the Handicapper General (H-G men, an allusion to the practice in the 1940s and 1950s of referring to Federal Bureau of Investigation and Secret Service officers as G-men, the G standing for government) enforce the equality laws.

People are made equal by devices which bring them down to the normalcy level in the story, which is actually below-average in intelligence, strength, and ability. These devices include weights to stunt speed and strength; masks, red rubber clown noses, or thick glasses to hide good looks and to make seeing difficult; and radio transmitters implanted in the ears of intelligent people, which emit sharp noises two or three times a minute to prevent sustained thought.

In April, described as "clammy" and driving "people crazy by not being springtime," H-G men take Harrison Bergeron—son of George and Hazel Bergeron—to jail on suspicion of plotting to overthrow the government. At the age of fourteen, seven-foot-tall Harrison is a genius and an athlete who bears heavier handicaps and more grotesque masking devices than anyone else. George and Hazel are watching a dance program on television and discussing George's handicaps, especially the different sounds transmitted to his mental handicap radio and the forty-seven pounds of birdshot in a canvas bag he wears around his neck. As a "normal" person who wears no handicaps, Hazel takes interest in the various sounds transmitted through George's radio. She also encourages George to remove a few lead balls from his handicap bag, at least just when he is home from work, to lighten his load. Hazel's suggestion to bend the rules leads George to defend their society and its laws.

A news bulletin announcing Harrison's escape from jail interrupts the dance program, followed soon thereafter by a live shot of Harrison breaking down the television studio door and addressing the dancers, musicians, and audience. He declares himself emperor, proclaiming that everyone must do what he says at once, and further asserts his superiority even with the significant handicaps he bears: "Even as I stand here—crippled, hobbled, sickened—I am a greater ruler than any man who ever lived! Now watch me become what I can become!" He tears off his handicaps, chooses one of the ballerinas as his empress, and proceeds, with her, to show people "the meaning of the word dance." In the process, they defy the laws of the land, the laws of gravity, and the laws of motion by leaping high enough to kiss the thirty-foot high ceiling. Remaining suspended in air a few inches below the ceiling, they linger over a long kiss which is interrupted by Handicapper General Diana Moon Glampers, who kills Harrison and the ballerina instantly with a double-blast of her shotgun. Hazel and George witness their son's death, but both forget why they are so sad immediately afterwards. George advises Hazel to forget sad things, and then the sound of a riveting gun in George's ear-radio leads them into a verbal exchange echoing comic lines popularized by comedians George Burns and Gracie Allen, from the closing dialogue of their television show.

George Bergeron

Harrison's father, George Bergeron, bears multiple government-imposed handicaps which repress his "way above-normal" intelligence. He refuses to remove any of them, however, for he believes that any attempt to change the present situation will inevitably cause civilization to regress back into the "dark ages," when there was competition. George and Hazel, his wife, witness Harrison's rebellious act on television, but afterwards cannot remember why they are sad. George wears birdshot weights and a mental handicap radio in his ear that receives a "sharp noise" transmission designed "to keep people . . . from taking unfair advantage of their brains."

Harrison Bergeron

Although he is only fourteen years old, the title character, Harrison Bergeron, stands seven feet tall and possesses an intelligence so immense that, at the beginning of the story, the Handicapper General has Harrison arrested "on suspicion of plotting to overthrow the government." Harrison escapes, however, and goes to the television station to publicly declare himself emperor. He selects a ballerina as his empress, and the two begin to dance. "[N]eutralizing gravity with love and pure will," the couple leap high enough to kiss the ceiling and remain suspended in mid air. At that moment, Diana Moon Glampers, the United States Handicapper General, blasts the couple out of the air with a "double-barreled ten-gauge shotgun," ending Harrison's life and his self-declared reign.

Harrison's actions suggest an ironic theme: corruptive power. Upon his escape, Harrison repeats government errors by establishing himself as the sole, nonelected, source of governmental authority. Had his rebellion succeeded, he would have forced people to break the law by making them remove their government-imposed handicaps. That act, according to Harrison's father, George, would send society back to the "dark ages" of social and individual competition.

Hazel Bergeron

Harrison's mother, Hazel Bergeron, does not need to wear any handicaps—mental or physical— as she possesses "normal" intelligence, appearance, and strength. In this story, however, "normal" entails that one is incompetent, or unable to fathom anything beyond that which is superficial. Hazel's dialogue with her husband, George, recalls the comedic team of George Burns and Gracie Allen.

Diana Moon Glampers

Although Diana Moon Glampers, the United States Handicapper General, appears briefly toward the end of the story in order to quell Harrison's rebellion by killing him, her presence pervades the story. As Handicapper General, she ruthlessly maintains law and order without due process. One of the few descriptions of her implies that Glampers herself is not "above normal."

Themes

Freedom

As a theme, freedom remains in the background of the story, emerging when Harrison escapes from jail. In the story's futuristic society, freedom is no longer a bedrock American value; enforcing the law that makes those who are "above normal" equal to those who are "normal" has become the major social value. Forced equality by handicapping the above-normal individuals evolved as a response to the demonized concept of competition (which existed in "the dark ages") in all its possible forms. Vonnegut suggests that freedom can be taken away relatively easily, especially since the forced equality in the story has been authorized by Amendments to the Constitution.

Civil Rights

Civil rights have become extinct in "Harrison Bergeron." The culture values mediocrity to the point that the people accept oppressive measures in the name of equality. Ironically, no one really benefits from these misguided attempts to enforce equality, except perhaps the incompetent, such as the television announcer who, "like all announcers, had a serious speech impediment." In Hazel's words, the announcer's incompetence should be forgiven because his attempt is "the big thing. He tried to do the best he could with what God gave him. He should get a nice raise for trying so hard." Should anyone in that society dare to become above average, he or she is immediately punished, as is Harrison, who is executed for shunning mediocrity and attempting to excel. By creating a society where the goal of equality has resulted in a grotesque caricature of humanity, Vonnegut implies that individual civil rights should never be sacrificed, not even for the alleged common good.

Knowledge and Ignorance

Everyone above average in any way has been forced by the government to bear a physical handicap that makes him or her "normal." People who are more intelligent or knowledgeable than the average person have had their knowledge subverted by such devices as the mental handicap ear radio. This device emits various noises every twenty seconds or so to prevent people from taking "unfair advantage of their brains." "Normal" in the story can best be described as subnormal, incompetent, and ignorant. Hazel is a case in point; as a normal person, she wears no handicaps, and she has a good heart, yet she knows very little about anything and cannot remember what she just saw or heard a moment ago. At the end of the story, she takes literally George's intensifying statement, "You can say that again," by repeating what she just said. Vonnegut suggests that an authoritarian government thrives on the ignorance of the people and on the suppression of intelligence and knowledge.

Law and Order

In addition to the critique of authoritarian government in the form of the Handicapper General agents (H-G men), Vonnegut discusses the ways in which the Handicapper General uses the fear of competition to make obeying the laws an ethical decision. Hazel feels sorry for George, who has to wear forty-seven pounds of birdshot around his neck, so she invites him to lighten his load. He rejects the idea of cheating (breaking the law) with a recital of the punishment: "two years in prison and two thousand dollars for every [lead birdshot] ball" taken out. He continues by describing the bandwagon effect: other people would try to break the law if George could do so. He asserts that backsliding would result in a return "to the dark ages, with everybody competing against everybody else." Cheating on laws, George claims (or is about to claim when a siren blast through his mental handicap radio shatters his concentration), would reduce society to chaos. Here, Vonnegut satirizes the fear of change and of uncertainty: victims of the oppressive law want to enforce it rather than take their chances without it.

Topics for Further Study

- Research the process by which proposed amendments to the United States Constitution pass Congress and are ratified into law. Based on what you find out, do you think it is likely that the Constitution will have 213 amendments in 2081 ? Why or why not?

- Investigate the controversy caused by Federal Communications Commission chairman Newton Minow's May, 1961, speech in which he labeled television "a vast wasteland." Compare Minow's historical commentary about television to current commentaries and note how much (or how little) has changed.

- Read the United States' founding documents—particularly the Declaration of Independence, the United States Constitution, or the Federalist Papers—to determine the promise of equality or lack thereof found within them. Compare the ideas found in these documents with those in documents associated with the Civil Rights Movement of the 1950s—particularly the 1954 U. S. Supreme Court decision in *Brown v. Board of Education*—and the early 1960s, particularly Martin Luther King's "Letter from Birmingham Jail" and his 1963 speech known as "I Have a Dream."

Strength and Weakness

One of the implied reasons Harrison may want to overthrow the government has to do with strength and weakness. He recognizes the inequality of forcing strong people (those mentally, intellectually, and physically strong) to give up their strength for an orderly society of equal, law-abiding citizens. Of course, the enforcers of the law do not have to submit to forced equality themselves; they have no handicaps, which could signify their inherent mediocrity, as does the implied physical resemblance of Hazel to Diana Moon Glampers, the

Handicapper General herself. Vonnegut shows what extraordinary strength can do: defy the laws of gravity and motion. But Vonnegut also shows that strength can be used to oppress the weak, even in the name of protecting the weak against the excesses of the strong.

Ubermensch ("Superman")

The idea of the superhuman materializes in the character of Harrison. Though only fourteen years old, at seven feet tall with a high intellect, he exceeds the physical and intellectual abilities of anyone else in the story. Likewise, his physical appearance, judged by the kinds of handicaps he must wear, suggests an Adonis-like figure. His handicaps include thick, wavy-lens spectacles; a red rubber clown nose; and snaggle-tooth black caps for his teeth. His natural abilities do not make him immortal, however; like other human beings, he can die from an antiquated weapon like the ten-gauge double-barreled shotgun of Diana Moon Glampers. Harrison's attempt to assert his authority neither lasts long nor has any real effect on anyone. Truly befitting the superman concept, he declares himself emperor, "a greater ruler than any man who ever lived" (even with his handicaps). He does not recognize, however, his human flaw: replacing one authoritarian government with another. Like so many other revolutions, Harrison's short-lived attempt to overthrow the ruthless totalitarianism that has become the American government becomes totalitarian itself. Vonnegut suggests that power, whether invested in the government or in the individual figure, corrupts.

American Dream

The American Dream, best described as upward social and economic class mobility through hard work and education has become an American Nightmare in "Harrison Bergeron." No one, except the Handicapper General agents, can achieve upward mobility, either because they bear artificial handicaps or because they are naturally mediocre. In a scheme that brings anyone who is above normal in *any* aspect down to the level of a person who is normal in *all* aspects, no one can dream about moving upward.

Media Influence

Vonnegut suggests the powerful influence of broadcast media in the story. Radio is the medium of the mental handicap noises used to prevent anyone with the ability to think from doing so. But television accomplishes the same thing for normal people like Hazel, who "had a perfectly average intelligence, which meant she couldn't think about anything except in short bursts." This lack of concentration has come to be known as short attention span, or attention deficit disorder. Many critics credit television for the decreasing attention span of the population. They also suggest television programming desensitizes people to real life, in part because it requires nothing of the viewer.

Significantly, approximately five months before publication of the story in 1961, Newton Minow, new chair of the Federal Communications Commission (a government agency that regulates broadcast media), called television a "vast wasteland" of mediocrity in programming. Vonnegut suggests the importance of television as a means of controlling information by having Harrison Bergeron take over the television studio and proclaim himself emperor. Vonnegut also shows the numbing influence of television by having Hazel forget what she has seen—her son's killing—even though she reacts by recognizing that something sad has happened.

Style

Setting

Setting the story 120 years in the future allows readers to more easily accept some of the more absurd events in "Harrison Bergeron." The actual physical location of the story does not matter and, therefore, is unknown. One glaring *anachronism*—a concept or an object not known or invented at the time of the story; or an object that belongs to a previous era—should be noted: the use of a shotgun. Readers might expect that some exotic form of weaponry would have been developed and used that far into the future. Similarly, the idea that 213 Amendments to the Constitution would have been ratified predicts a radical change in American legislation. At the time the story was written, only twenty-four amendments had been passed by the Congress and ratified by the states, the first ten of which (known as the Bill of Rights) became law in 1791. In the 170 years between 1791 and the time the story was written, only fourteen additional amendments had been ratified. Ironically, the 211th, 212th, and 213th Amendments of the story restrict the civil rights of most people, as opposed to the amendments over the first two hundred years of the nation.

Point of View

The story is told in the third-person-limited point of view; the narrator is not a character in the story, but he is privy to the thoughts of one character. Readers are allowed to know what George Bergeron is thinking, as when he "was toying with the vague notion that maybe dancers shouldn't be handicapped." The events in "Harrison Bergeron" are related by an objective narrator. The narrator does not draw conclusions, make decisions, or make judgments about the events. The objectivity of the narrator suggests a distancing from the hostile world of the story.

Satire and Black Humor

The story uses satire and a kind of humor known as black humor. The humor mostly involves George and Hazel, although the appearance of Harrison (red rubber nose, artificially snaggle-toothed, three hundred pounds of handicaps) can be seen as comical. George and Hazel's dialogue at the end of the story alludes to comics George Burns and Gracie Allen, who had a popular television show in the late 1950s and early 1960s. At the end of each show, George and Gracie performed a stand-up routine related to that night's episode. Often, George would say to Gracie, "You can say that again," and she would reply the same way Hazel replies to George Bergeron: She would literally repeat what she had just said. Gracie Allen's comic persona mirrors Hazel's persona; both seem somewhat scatterbrained. The humorous dialogue between Hazel and George Bergeron could be considered black humor, which has proved difficult to define. Related to both sick humor (making fun of, say, a person's disability) and gallows humor (people laughing in the midst of helplessness), as well as the absurd (so far-fetched as to be nearly implausible), black humor can incorporate all of these characteristics. It can be defined as the juxtaposition of pain and laughter, unusual fact and calmly inadequate reactions, and cruelty and tenderness. The ending dialogue between Hazel and George juxtaposes all three of those pairs, as Hazel and George have just witnessed the killing of their son. Satire, ridiculing a person, place, or idea with the notion of effecting change, always involves morality. Here, Vonnegut satirizes the notion of handicapping people to enforce equality, the failure of rebellion, the apathy engendered in people who watch television, and authoritarian government. As Conrad Festa claims in *Vonnegut in America,*

> Stories such as "Harrison Bergeron" . . . fit easily and recognizably into the satiric genre. That is, they (1) sustain a reductive attack on their objects, (2) convey to their intended readers significances at odds with the literal or surface meanings, and (3) are pervaded and dominated by various satiric techniques.

Allusion

Vonnegut uses several allusions—references to

people, historical events, and other literature outside the text—in "Harrison Bergeron." The month of April, which "still drove people crazy by not being springtime," is doubly allusive, initially referring to the first line of T. S. Eliot's 1922 poem, *The Waste Land*: "April is the crulest month. . . ." The second allusion derived from April stems from the first: the title of the poem also serves in part as the title of a 1961 speech by then Federal Communications Commission Chair Newton Minow, referring to television as "a vast wasteland." The abbreviation of the Handicapper-General agents, "H-G men," ironically alludes to the abbreviation "G-men" (for government agents; i.e., Secret Service agents, FBI agents). Generally, these government agents were held in high esteem, unlike the H-G men, until the 1960s and 1970s, when their activities came into legal and ethical question. The allusion of Diana Moon, the Handicapper General's first and middle names, refers to the Roman goddess of the hunt, Diana, who is associated with the moon. Diana was known for her vengeance, which could explain the ruthless killing of Harrison Bergeron in the story. Thor, identified in the story as the god of thunder, was, in Norse mythology, the oldest and most powerful son of Odin, king of the gods. He possessed great strength and skill in fighting. This allusion serves to underscore Harrison's strength without his handicaps. There is an indirect reference to cartoonist Rube Goldberg, which highlights the absurdity of the handicapping technology, especially for such a futuristic story. Rube Goldberg's cartoons generally depicted elaborate schemes to accomplish the simplest tasks. For instance, instead of an alarm clock, Goldberg might construct a chain of events from the sun reflecting light onto a bird, which might then peck at a string, which would then release a bowling ball that would trip a lever, opening a door to a rooster cage, allowing the rooster to emerge and signal an alarm with his crowing. The more complex these mechanisms are, the funnier. Thus, the various handicaps described in the story seem much like Rube Goldberg cartoons, and seem humorous to readers who recognize the allusion. The final allusion is to the comedy team of George Burns and Gracie Allen, and to their television show. The dialogue at the end of the story reflects similar dialogues at the end of the "Burns and Allen" television show. Gracie, who played a scatterbrain, would indeed repeat lines when George used the phrase, "You can say that again," just as Hazel Bergeron does in the story. Television's role in the story is to numb, desensitize, or otherwise occupy the time of citizens, and to prevent sustained thought on the part of those of normal intelligence.

The Modern Civil Rights Movement

In the late 1940s progress, albeit in fits and starts, began to occur in the movement toward full civil rights for African Americans in the United States. Beginning with Jackie Robinson, major league baseball began the process of integration, as did the military in the late 1940s. In the 1954 case known as *Brown v. Board of Education of Topeka,* the United States Supreme Court decided that the doctrine of "separate but equal" facilities set forth in the 1896 *Plessy v. Ferguson* case no longer held true. A year later, the Supreme Court ordered lower courts to use "all deliberate speed" in desegregating the public schools. In the Deep South, governors, state legislatures, and local school boards resisted, in some cases passing laws to try to thwart the ruling. In addition to the landmark Supreme Court ruling, an African-American woman named Rosa Parks refused to give up her seat in the front of a Montgomery, Alabama, bus to sit in the back as a local ordinance required. Her subsequent arrest led to a boycott of downtown businesses by African Americans. It also gave the Reverend Martin Luther King, Jr., an opportunity to begin his crusade for civil rights long denied African Americans in the South. In September, 1957, President Dwight Eisenhower had to call out the Arkansas National Guard, as well as regular Army troops, to enforce desegregation of Little Rock, Arkansas, schools. In February, 1960, four African-American students began what became known as "sit-ins" when they sat down at a lunch counter for whites only in Greensboro, North Carolina. Sit-ins became a standard tactic in the civil rights movement, as was also true of the "Freedom Rides" (busloads of whites and African Americans who came to the South to help support voter registration drives and other civil rights activities) which began in 1961, the year "Harrison Bergeron" was published. Also in 1960, the U. S. Congress passed another civil rights act that allowed federal authorities to ensure that states allowed African Americans the unfettered right to register to vote. Even though the civil rights movement does not specifically relate to "Harrison Bergeron," it stands in the background as being one of the compelling public issues of the time. Vonnegut's use of the issue of equality in the story ignores the racial context on the surface, but it clearly invokes the fears of many, mostly white citizens who feared the federal government would in some way propose schemes that would enforce equality of outcome. Many apparently felt that desegregating the public schools and other facilities amounted to the same kind of tyranny exposed in the story.

The Cold War and Communism

The kind of government authority seen in "Harrison Bergeron" both mimics and satirizes the way Americans came to see the enemy—

socialism/communism and, specifically, the Soviet Union (USSR)—during the Cold War, which was near its height of distrust and fear in the late 1950s and early 1960s. Schools in different states introduced courses such as Communism vs. Americanism during the 1950s to wage the propaganda war at home. The fear of nuclear war led thousands of Americans to build bomb shelters in their backyards. Following Soviet Premier Nikita Khrushchev's promise to "bury" the United States in the late 1950s, significant fear of an authoritarian government taking over the so-called free world intensified in America. Communism as practiced in the USSR and in China meant a tyrannical rule without due process of law enforced by secret police and informers, similar to the way the United States is portrayed in the story. Making the fear more ominous and close to home was Fidel Castro's successful rebellion in Cuba, ending in 1959. By the middle of 1960, Americans realized that Castro was building a socialist state allied with and supported by the USSR. An attempt by the Soviet Union to station missiles in Cuba led to the Cuban Missile Crisis in 1962. Trade sanctions against Cuba began in 1960 and continue in the late 1990s. The paranoid climate caused by the establishment of a communist government a mere ninety miles from the United States sent many citizens into panic. Vonnegut recognized that the way communism was practiced led to the failure of its basic promise of providing a workers' paradise of equality in a classless society.

Compare & Contrast

- **1964:** President Lyndon B. Johnson signs the Civil Rights Act of 1964 into law. Title VII of the Act establishes The Equal Employment Opportunities Commission, which prohibits discrimination in employment on the basis of race, sex, national origin, and religion.

  Late 1990s: Affirmative action programs, which set guidelines for preferred hiring of minority and women workers and students, come under fire. Businesses and universities are sued for reverse discrimination by whites passed over for various positions and promotions.

- **1950s:** The CIA experiments with various forms of mind control, including testing LSD, a hallucinogen, as a truth serum on U.S. soldiers.

  1993: Rumors surface that the FBI is considering using an acoustic mind control device during a standoff with cult leader David Koresh in Waco, Texas. The device, developed by a Russian scientist, is supposedly capable of placing thoughts in a person's mind without the person's knowledge of the source of the thoughts.

- **1960s:** Young people unite in unprecedented numbers to protest the Vietnam War, racism, and sexual discrimination. Vonnegut's writings become very popular in this politically active era.

  1990s: "Hate crime" legislation provides stiffer penalties for those convicted of harassment and other crimes directed at people based on their ethnicity, sexual orientation, and physical or mental disabilities. Critics say the laws criminalize thought rather than action, and that punishment varies according to the characteristics of the victim.

Television and American Culture

One of the few scholarly mentions of "Harrison Bergeron" occurs in Robert Uphaus's essay, "Expected Meanings in Vonnegut's Dead-End Fiction." Uphaus identifies the basis of the catastrophe known as the United States government in 2081: television. He asserts, "The history of mankind, Vonnegut implies in the story, is a history of progressive desensitization partly spurred on by the advent of television." Coincidentally, then newly appointed chair of the Federal

Communications Commission, Newton Minow, delivered an attack on television five months before "Harrison Bergeron" was published. In the speech, Minow called television "a vast wasteland" of destructive or meaningless programs. Minow claimed that instead of challenging people to think, television programming was making it easier for people to avoid serious thought. The story clearly uses television as a time filler, a method of preventing average people from thinking, similar to Minow's description. Hazel Bergeron best illustrates this point. Although of "perfectly average intelligence," she has such a short attention span that she is prevented from remembering why she cries at "Something real sad [she saw] on television": the murder of her son, Harrison. While Vonnegut aims his satiric barbs at overreaching, authoritarian government, television equally bears the brunt of his attack for its role in the erosion of thought. Vonnegut suggests that television serves the same purpose for normal people that the mental handicap radios serve for those above normal in intelligence.

World War II

Vonnegut's skepticism of government power and of scientific solutions to problems comes from his experiences in World War II. Specifically, he was disillusioned by the lies told in the name of winning the war and by the mass destruction caused by application of scientific discoveries to weaponry. As a prisoner of war, Vonnegut survived the Allied bombing raids on Dresden, Germany, in February, 1945. There, over 135,000 people—mostly civilians—died from the bombing, more than the total killed by both atomic bombs dropped on Hiroshima and Nagasaki, Japan, later that year. Vonnegut has recounted this story in various places, most notably his 1969 novel *Slaughterhouse-Five, or the Children's Crusade*. In his 1991 autobiographical collage, *Fates Worse Than Death,* Vonnegut reprints a directory carried aboard British and American bombers in World War II showing "there wasn't much in the Dresden area worth bombing out of business according to our Intelligence experts." The reason Vonnegut harps on this issue is that the Dresden raids were kept secret from the public for almost twenty years, and then were defended by the claim that Dresden contained targets of military importance. He notes that this act and the subsequent secrecy disillusioned him about his government. This realization that the government can and does lie to its citizens, for ill or for good, serves as the premise for distrust of government power in "Harrison Bergeron."

Critical Overview

The first critical responses to "Harrison Bergeron" did not appear until 1968, when the story was reprinted in Vonnegut's collection *Welcome to the Monkey House*. Many reviewers, like Larry L. King in *New York Times Book Review,* who called the collection "old soup," were decidedly unenthusiastic. Some of the stories had already been published in an earlier collection titled *Canary in a Cat House* (1961), and others had been first published in commercial, "slick" magazines, thus bringing into question their literary value. Criticizing "Harrison Bergeron," King claimed, "I know nothing of Mr. Vonnegut's personal politics, but extant Goldwaterites or Dixiecrats might read into this the ultimate horrors of any further extension of civil-rights or equal-opportunity laws." The term *Goldwaterites* refers to admirers of former Arizona Senator Barry Goldwater, the 1964 Republican candidate for President, who was known as "Mr. Conservative." The term *Dixiecrats* refers to white Southerners who stood strongly (and sometimes violently) against extending civil rights to African Americans throughout the 1950s and 1960s. In fact, by the time of King's review, political conservatives who stood against federal government civil rights laws had already appropriated the story for William F. Buckley's *National Review* magazine (November 16, 1965). King's early review identified what has become one of the most controversial aspects of the story: how the story can easily be read as a criticism of measures advocated by minorities and women to ensure equality. Vonnegut pokes fun at the absurd and extreme steps taken to ensure equality in the futuristic society, with cumbersome low-technology handicaps forced on above-average citizens upon pain of severe punishment. "Harrison Bergeron" has been used more recently to illustrate the conflict between the American political ideology of equality and the practice of discrimination based on superficial traits such as race and gender. In 1982 political conservatives again used "Harrison Bergeron" to oppose affirmative action and other social programs: a book published by Canada's Fraser Institute in 1982, *Discrimination, Affirmative Action, and Equal Opportunity: An Economic and Social Perspective,* used the story as the title for its last chapter.

Some early reviewers of *Welcome to the Monkey House,* such as Charles Nicol in the *Atlantic Monthly* and Michael Levitas in the *New York Times,* ignored "Harrison Bergeron." Other critics, such as Gerard Reedy in *America,* focused on the title character as an "all-American boy," and compared Vonnegut's character to similar characters created by other contemporary authors such as John Updike and Philip Roth. Reedy found that Vonnegut, in contrast to the other authors, was "not as serious" in his "satire of American types," and "[a] social critic only by indirection." Levitas's review, like King's, focused on the recycled nature of the commercial stories. Quoting Vonnegut's own introduction, in which he commented, "Here one finds the fruits of Free Enterprise," Levitas paraphrased Lamont Cranston (the original title character of the radio show *The Shadow*) by claiming "the seeds of Free Enterprise bear bitter fruit." Charles Nicol at least mentioned "Vonnegut's special enemies," some of which surface as themes in "Harrison Bergeron": "science, morality, free enterprise, socialism, fascism, Communism, any force in our lives which regards human beings as ciphers."

The story's outward focus on the idea of equality forced by law has made it a popular choice for high school and college literature anthologies, even though the story itself has received little scholarly attention. Vonnegut's literary reputation rests more on his novels than on his short fiction, and Vonnegut himself has said he wrote stories to earn money so could work on his novels. Many reviewers of *Welcome to the Monkey House* agree with Vonnegut's apparent devaluation of the stories.

Sources

Frye, Northrop. "The Nature of Satire," in *University of Toronto Quarterly,* Vol. 14, October, 1944.

King, Larry L. "Old Soup," in *New York Times Book Review,* September 1, 1968, pp. 4-5, 19.

Levitas, Mitchel. "Books of the Times: A Slight Case of Candor," in *New York Times,* August 19, 1968, p. 35.

Meek, Martha (revised by Peter Reed). "Kurt Vonnegut, Jr.," in *Critical Survey of Short Fiction,* revised edition, Vol. 6, edited by Frank Magill, Salem Press, 1993, pp. 2364-71.

Minow, Newton. "The Vast Wasteland," reprinted in *The Annals of America, Vol. 18, 1961-1968: The Burdens of World Power,* Encyclopaedia Britannica, 1968, pp. 12-20.

Nichol, Charles. "The Volunteer Fireman," in *Atlantic Monthly,* Vol. 222, No. 3., September, 1968, pp. 123—4.

Reedy, Gerard. Review of *Welcome to the Monkey House,* in *America,* Vol. 119, No. 7, September 14, 1968, pp. 190-91.

Schatt, Stanley. "The Short Stories," in *Kurt Vonnegut, Jr.,* Boston: Twayne, 1976, pp. 119-35.

Uphaus, Robert W. "Expected Meaning in Vonnegut's Dead-End Fiction," in *The Critical*

Response to Kurt Vonnegut, edited by Leonard Mustazza, Westport, Conn.: Greenwood Press, 1994, pp. 165-74.

Vonnegut, Kurt. "Address to P.E.N. Conference in Stockholm, 1973," in his *Wampeters, Foma, & Granfalloons: Opinions,* New York: Dell, 1974, pp. 225-29.

Vonnegut, Kurt. "America: What's Good, What's Bad?" *inVogue,* Vol. 162, July, 1973, 62-64. Reprinted as "Address at Rededication of Wheaton College Library" in his *Wampeters, Foma, & Granfalloons: Opinions,* New York: Dell, 1974, pp. 225-29.

Vonnegut, Kurt. *Fates Worse Than Death: An Autobiographical Collage of the 1980s,* New York: G. P. Putnam's Sons, 1991, pp. 82-5, 113-16, 149-52.

Vonnegut, Kurt. "Mark Twain," in his *Palm Sunday: An Autobiographical Collage,* New York: Delacorte Press, 1981, pp. 166-72.

Vonnegut, Kurt. "Playboy Interview," in *Playboy,* Vol. 20, July, 1973, pp. 57-60+. Reprinted in his *Wampeters, Foma, & Granfalloons: Opinions,* New York: Dell, 1974, pp. 237-85.

Further Reading

The Annals of America, Vol. 17, 1950-1960: Cold War in the Nuclear Age, Encyclopaedia Britannica, 1968.

> The volume features important events and their dates in a chronology, as well as reprints of original speeches and documents Klinkowitz, Jerome, and Donald L. Lawler, eds. *Vonnegut in America: An Introduction to the Life and Work of Kurt Vonnegut,* Delacorte Press-Seymour Lawrence, 1977, 304 p.

> Includes Conrad Festa's perceptive essay on Vonnegut as a satirist and a complete bibliography of Vonnegut's works.

Klinkowitz, Jerome, Lawler, Donald L., and John Somer, eds. *The Vonnegut Statement,* Delacorte Press, 1973, 286 p.

> Explores Vonnegut's public and personal life, as well as the novels. Klinkowitz proposes that Vonnegut represents middle-class, rather than rebellious values.

Layman, Richard, ed. *American Decades: 1950-1959, Vol. 6,* Manly, Inc.-Gale Research, 1994.

> Provides information on events from

the 1950s, classified into such categories as "Government and Politics," "Law and Justice," and "Lifestyles and Social Trends."

Layman, Richard, ed. *American Decades: 1960-1969, Vol. 7,* Manly, Inc.-Gale Research, 1994.

> Provides information on the 1960s, classified into such categories as "Government and Politics," "Law and Justice," and "Lifestyles and Social Trends."

Leeds, Marc. *The Vonnegut Encyclopedia: An Authorized Compendium,* Greenwood Press, 1995, 693 p.

> This alphabetically arranged encyclopedia contains entries on everything from Celia Aamons (from *Cat's Cradle*) to Zog (a Kilgore Trout character from *Breakfast of Champions*).

Merrill, Robert, ed. *Critical Essays on Kurt Vonnegut,* G. K. Hall, 1990, 235 p.

> Includes reviews of Vonnegut's novels; discussions of his early works; an extended section of essays on *Slaughterhouse-Five;* and discussions of the later works.

Mustazza, Leonard, ed. *The Critical Response to Kurt Vonnegut,* Greenwood Press, 1994, 346 p.

> This collection of essays, original

reviews of books, and excerpts from other books traces the scholarly reputation of Vonnegut over the years. Most published Vonnegut scholars are represented, as are such writers as Michael Crichton, John Irving, Doris Lessing, and Terry Southern.